I see a gossamer thread glistening in the fire's light,

I hear the rowing of a boat in the harbour,

the Northern Lights rise against the northern sky.

Oh, I give thanks by my immortal soul

that it is I who am sitting here!

Knut Hamsun (1859-1952)

Hugeltårnet near Efjord

I feel the Earth's axis tilt.

I can see the sun again.

I sing a Sami song.

Ailo Gaup

Børvasstindan

At break of day
the wonder ensues:
the Sun's orb is raised
by hands unknown

above the horizon,
set free then sways
up towards heaven.

In reverential hope then
all life falls silent:

nature trembles
on Transfiguration's Mount.

Vilhelm Krag (1871-1923)

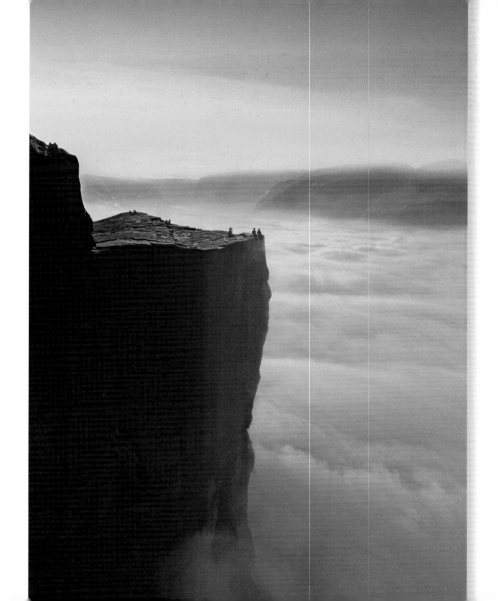

Like myriad suns how it shines,

stars and clouds of gold!

See how each sun-touched gully

a full complement holds!

This gold, pure white and flaming red

streaming from the sky

shouts exulting heavenwards

that life shall never die.

Gunnar Reiss-Andersen (1896-1964)

Preikestolen / The Pulpit Rock

Help me, singing light of the day
to find the word, the creating word,
help me, night's embracing shade
life's depths to fathom, its mystic code.
Help me, you loving human eyes
to mount on souls to the souls' abode.

Sigbjørn Obstfelder (1866-1900)

Kjeragbolten / The Kjerag Boulder, Lysefjorden

Skoddeberg near Grovfjord

Portrait

You stand
in the borderland
between day and night
at the diurnal crux –
this contrastful
tremulous moment
of clarifying light and
consuming dark

Ragnhild N. Grødal

On frost-green sky over mountain peaks,

play tongues of fire.

Night of yearning.

Aurora night.

Flickering searchlights probe inwards – inwards

to the endless, unplumbed spaces.

Jan Magnus Bruheim (1914-1988)

Rapadalen, Sarek

Thanksgiving

Praise to the light
of the world in my mind,
the sun's rising
and the gift of sight!
From embers under ashes
the fire re-awakes.
Joy lives anew
at the wonder of the day.

Johannes V. Jensen (1873-1950)

Then come, let's light small lights for one another,
fires to ward off night in a wintry world

where the frost will yield when our human warmth
reaches through the darkness — like lights along a fjord.

Helge Stangnes

Trollfjorden

In the west hang the dying traces
of the sun's evening rays,
and clouds on clouds, like angel hosts,
with rosy face and golden wings,
lie gathered all ablaze.
In the east awaits the shining moon,
and the swooning day sinks gently down
from the radiant mountainsides.

J. S. Welhaven (1807-1873)

Sunshine always brings news.
Where is there a fresher pleasure
than that which tastes of dew,
light cleans it up in the early hours,
it's dipped in moisture,
posted on the wall,
and always right on target,
a new day blazons forth!

Stein Mehren

The midnight sun at Hamarøy

Austnesfjorden, Lofoten

There a great hilltop towers

with its coronet of snow

and bedecked in new leaves

shines from waters below.

And it smiles at the shore

with its breast all afire

on this summer eve so still:

I remember, remember so well this great hill!

Elias Blix (1836-1902)

Rafsundet, Lofoten

A sun-filled day over summer leaves,

a song, rippling so softly.

shimmering water and a silver-bright cloud,

a lone spring murmuring,

two sparkling eyes, unruly locks,

a mouth, laughing up at me...

Whose were those eyes, whose that hair,

and whose those cherry lips? –

Vilhelm Krag (1871-1923)

Torghatten

Awakening

Here comes the sun from its
night-shelter, here glides the light

gossamer-soft over the hills, here
comes the day like an exquisite gift,

a wide-awake clearness all around, here
comes the sun and lights up

a myriad colours, entices
all that grows out of night and sleep,

here comes a tiny
morning cloud, here comes the light.

Tove Lie

Once evenings were full
of the wind and water's rush.
Now a long-forgotten sound
vibrates between us.

Tor Jonsson (1916-1951)

Piping winds, bird cries
all summer long.
Skerries, skerries –
shores with kelp strewn…

Lighthearted summer days,

nights under starry skies,

summers in song!

Rolf Hiorth-Schøyen (1887-1932)

I am beautiful, for I have grown
in the garden of my beloved.
I stood in the spring rain and drank of desire,
I stood in the sun and drank of fire –
now I stand open, waiting.

Edith Södergran (1892-1923)

Høvåg, Lillesand

Don't give me the whole truth,

don't bring me the ocean for my thirst,

don't give me heaven when I ask for light,

but give me a glimpse, a drop, a speck,

as birds carry dew drops from leaves

and the wind a grain of salt.

Olav H. Hauge (1908-1994)

Each day should be consumed like a bonfire of dreams,
and burn to the ground with no wish fulfilled.

And always you yearn for the things that are far,
but remember that Earth too is a star!

Arnulf Øverland (1889–1968)

Friends are few and far between.

Between friends are many acquaintances,

much casual talk.

Friends are like lights from distant houses

in the wilderness's cavernous night.

You can't mistake them.

Kolbein Falkeid

Gravvatn, Sirdal

Sky, you're blushing faintly red,
where the sun has been lost to view.

Sky, that calm look on your face
is ruffled lightly by your broad,
magnanimous smile.

Sigbjørn Obstfelder (1866-1900)

Moments

life's young innocents

blossom around us.

Reality

balances on the sound wave from a word in space.

The tree is born when we look at it.

Everything is now.

Kolbein Falkeid

It's morning again, little hope
and the world's drying off with
fresh-laundered sunshine.
Life's face is never the same
though we may look at it for all eternity.

Kolbein Falkeid

Light

Light is everything in the world

to men's eyes

Light thirsts after light

Yes, the soul, twin to the stars

travels through space

to find, be made eternal by light

and grasps, trembling,

the Sun

a torch handed on

from runner to runner

through the millennia!

Gunvor Hofmo (1921-1995)

THE NORDIC LIGHT - NEW EDITION 2010

Text and picture selection: Snorre Aske, Jens-Uwe Kumpch
Idea and layout: Natur og Kulturforlaget
English translations, except where attributed below: E. Fraser

Source references:

Knut Hamsun, Pan, Gyldendal 2002, English translation published by Alkin Books Ltd., Windmill Grove, 1994, transl. James W. McFarlane

Ailo Gaup, Jeg lager en joik, in: I stallos natt, Gyldendal 1984

Gunnar Reiss-Andersen, Sommer, in: Norsk lyrikk gjennom tusen år, Aschehoug 1950

Ragnhild N. Grødal, Portrett, in: Tråder i livsveven, Cappelen 1999

J.M. Bruheim, Brevet til kjærligheten (excerpt), Aschehoug 1977

Helge Stangnes, Lyset langs en fjord. Nordkalott-Forlaget 1992

Stein Mehren, Snakke solskinn (excerpt), in: Tidsalder, Aschehoug 1966

Tove Lie, Oppvåkning, in: Paradis Sonate, Aschehoug 1980

Tor Jonsson, Når du er borte (excerpt), from: Ei dagbok for mitt hjarte, Noregs boklag 1951

Olav H. Hauge, Kom ikkje med heile sanningi, in: Dikt i samling, Det norske samlaget 1994 transl. Olav Grinde

Arnulf Øverland, Til en misantrop (excerpt), Samlede dikt 1911-1940, Aschehoug 1999

Kolbein Falkeid, (p. 38) from: Opp- og utbrudd (1978), in: Samlede dikt, Cappelen 2003
(p. 42), from: Gjenskinn, in: Samlede dikt, Cappelen 2003
Morgen (p. 44), in: De store strendenes samtale, Dikt i utvalg, Cappelen 1998

Gunvor Hofmo, Nabot, from: Samlede dikt, Gyldendal 1996

Photographers: Snorre Aske / www.naturkultur.no, p. 6 – 16 - 20 – 22 – 28 – 30 – 36 – 40
Henning Pettersen / www.naturkultur.no, p. 8 – 32, www.nettfoto.no, p. 10 – 12 – 38, Sven Halling, p. 14
Aune Forlag, p. 18 – 24, Per Eide Studio, p. 26, Asgeir Helgesen / NN / Samfoto, p. 34, Thor Østbye, p. 42
Bård Løken / NN / Samfoto, p. 44, Jan Arvid Dale / NN / Samfoto, cover, www.jervfoto.no, p. 2
Tor Egil Kvalnes, p. 4, Joshua Stang, p. 46